Motivating Adolescent Readers Using Fluency and Prosody Instruction

Marta Whittington, Ed.D

July, 2013

Words of Wisdom Educational Consulting

Dedication

This work is dedicated to my strong literacy team: Casey, Donna, Kelly, and Hilary. Teaching reading and writing to a diverse K-12 population takes hard work, determination, and a true commitment to those students. Your efforts are noted and appreciated every day.

ISBN: 978-1490963501

Words of Wisdom wishes to thank Dr. Whittington for her tireless work with students. She has served in many capacities in her career, and her work has always proven to be top notch as the reader is about to discover.

Motivating Adolescent Readers Using

Fluency and Prosody Instruction

Something is drastically wrong when our students are silenced by texts. I suspect this is often the result of problematic instruction. For too long, children have read literature and then faced a barrage of questions, each with one right answer. (Lucy Calkins, 1999, p. 13)

Why Fluency and Prosody Instruction are Necessary and Important

It is impossible to discuss fluency instruction for adolescent learners without keeping the end results in mind. The goal of all literacy instruction must be the deep comprehension of complex reading structures these students will face as they progress through middle school and into high school. Today's adolescent students will encounter multiple genres of text each day, and they must be equipped with the basic tools with which to read and understand the technical language of math and science, then immediately switch gears to discuss literature. And, they must be able to do all of this with the goal of reaching Common Core State Standard (CCSS) level of synthesizing the information in order to be able to discuss and argue accordingly in these multiple genres, using evidence from the text to support their arguments and writing.

Middle and high school teachers have no easy job. They are expected to take a group of diverse readers and writers who have needs ranging from weak word analysis skills to high level evidence-based critical thinking, yet these teachers are expected to move all students through text that is more complex and demanding than any they have ever before encountered. The needs of adolescent learners are multifaceted and, for the first time in their lives, these students are expected to perform with independence they have never before experienced, while concurrently learning to structure their own time and academics. A lack of advanced reading skills for many students leads to well-justified cause for concern among educators, particularly regarding adolescent students who are disengaged or struggling readers (Alvermann, 2005).

Teachers of content areas such as math, science, and social studies, are, for perhaps the first time, being required to implement instruction of reading skills in order to help students utilize the science, history, and math reading standards that are outlined in CCSS. With such rapidly changing accountability and standards, many middle and high school teachers are being forced to move out of their subject area comfort zone as they integrate reading strategies and writing instruction to support the content material in their classes.

Two problems are emerging: the text material continues to become increasingly more difficult each school year for students to read and understand, so the skill level they had developed in the elementary grades may be insufficient; and, teachers report that they do not have the time nor the expertise in literacy instruction to be able to support adolescent readers who struggle with this complex text (Kamil, Borman, Dole, Kral, Salinger, & Torgesen, 2008).

How can increasing fluency skill support students' literacy across all areas of the middle school curriculum? Although the National Reading Panel recommended in 2000 that fluency be included in best practice reading instruction, this area of instruction has been underutilized for many decades, (Allington, 2000). Becoming a fluent reader increases---or is the result of-----multiple sub-skills working together. However, most reading skills are not detached processes that work alone. Most specific reading skills are intertwined and interdependent, and it is impossible to break these into separate parts. For example, one result of increased fluency is more accurate and faster word recognition, called automaticity. Increased automaticity results in smoother reading, which results in stronger comprehension and increased confidence. Improved comprehension and confidence, in turn, result in stronger motivation. The process is involved and cyclical, but the encouraging thing to note is that improving the fluency process is not extremely difficult or time consuming to support and improve. The results are strong: increased fluency yields a lot of bang for the buck. There is a growing body of research (Pressley, Gaskins, & Fingeret, 2006; Rasinski, Rikli,, & Johnston, 2009; Samuels, 1979; Schwanenflugel, Meisinger, Wisenbaker, & Kuhn, 2006) supporting the theory that reading fluency and prosody have a significant impact on reading and comprehension.

However, in order to fully understand the value of fluency intervention, educators must undergo a paradigm shift in their understanding of what teaching of reading involves. Reading is not a base set of skills a student either has or does not have, such as finding the main idea of a selection; nor is reading a skill that is learned in elementary school that follows a person throughout his lifetime. Simply stated, reading is a continuing set of strategies a person learns to use when he needs help decoding and understanding unfamiliar text at any stage of life. Reading strategies are much like tools you might find in a toolbox (Harvey & Goudvis, 2005) that a student can pull out to use when he needs them to do the specific job, or task, at hand. Different types of reading require different skills, and this "learning to read" process must follow a person throughout his lifetime as he encounters different types and different levels of text that he must decode and understand (Tovani, 2000).

Robb (2002) has challenged the myth among educators that "Learning to Read" happens in the early grades (K-3) and consists primarily of word analysis in decoding and memorizing basic sight words, while "Reading to Learn" begins in fourth grade and consists mostly of reading for information. Robb points out these practices aren't working, and research has clearly indicated for readers of all ages, that learning to read and reading to learn should be happening simultaneously and continuously, from preschool through middle and high school, and on into adulthood as complex reading demands increase with the subject material. Therefore, teachers of adolescent readers must sharpen a skill-set that will enhance their role in helping students learn to navigate the harder context material they face in middle and high school.

The bigger picture is that literacy is more than just reading and writing. Literacy includes all the ways a student is able to receive information and in turn communicates information to others. Literacy includes the sub-skills of receptive language, which are ways information is received such as hearing, reading, or observing. Literacy also includes the sub-skills of expressive language as the process of communicating information to others in ways such as speaking, writing, demonstrating, or drawing symbols. For students to have a deep understanding of content material they must be able to read, analyze, and write responsively while justifying an argument, and these skills must be learned by practicing and experiencing language in high level receptive and expressive situations (Beers, 2002).

Comprehension, or understanding what is being read, is the critical objective of all reading instruction. However, comprehension itself is not a finite skill that is black and white; present or not present. Rather, comprehension is a process. All readers, even adult readers, must learn to adjust the use of reading skills necessary for the reading task before them in order to gain understanding, and, as the reading material changes, so must the use of the tools of comprehension. For example, when a very proficient adult reader is faced with the task of reading and understanding an unfamiliar legal document such as a mortgage contract or a technical manual filled with unfamiliar text structures or vocabulary, he or she must work at a different level to decode the technical language and understand the difficult material than he would use for a piece of fictional literature read for pleasure.

Reports of reading deficits are prompting middle school administrators and teachers to search for instructional methods to meet the challenge of providing for these less than proficient readers (Duffy & Hoffman, 1999). Unfortunately, many districts are seeking commercial programs that claim to be a quick fix. There is a concerted effort among literacy leaders (Allington, 2007; Beers, 2002, Fisher & Ivey, 2006), to caution against putting too much emphasis on a particular program that is touted to be able to address the varied needs of all adolescent readers. Nichols, Rupley and Rasinski (2009) wrote: *It can be said that reading programs never rise above the quality of the instruction found within them* (p.1). Fisher and Ivey (2006) explained that although many programs differentiate materials and assignments for students, or have them work alone at a computer, that does not necessarily mean the student is getting instruction that is personalized to his needs and changes as he moves along the growth continuum.

Allington (2007) declared that it is inconceivable that any No Child Left Behind Response To Intervention plan would supply every student with a set of lessons from a single packaged program, because this is the sort of one-size-fits-all reading instruction that may have created the reading problem in the first place. These researchers advocate that students work with a well-trained teacher who is available to make split-second decisions as needed to facilitate student's understandings of reading strategies. The International Reading Association and the National Middle School Association (2001) support this focus on the teacher as the differentiating factor for student achievement, specifically noting that outstanding teachers can assess students' progress and immediately select instruction related to research based best practices. Excellent teachers have a large repertoire of methods to use in teaching reading, provide a range of materials and texts for children to read, and can tailor instruction to individual students.

The goal is to equip each student with the necessary metacognition tools and comprehension strategy tools so he can successfully navigate any and all reading text he will encounter in authentic reading situations (Harvey & Goudvis, 2005). Researcher Beers (2002) noted that, while gaining skill in an isolated program may increase a student's aptitude for that particular skill, there is no evidence this will make the student a better or more motivated reader.

This chapter outlines how the use of fluency and prosody instruction can provide teachers with ways to help students to become stronger and more confident readers who are better able to read and understand the content material, and will include ways to help motivate disengaged readers.

Fluent Reading Defined

Defining fluency is somewhat difficult because it has gained new meanings in recent years. Fluency is most often defined as the ability to read with a smooth speed, while using correct expression and phrasing. However, the current use of fluency in Response To Intervention (RTI) Curriculum Based Measurement (CBM) benchmark scoring has defined fluency as the calculation of words correct per minute. This practice of focusing exclusively on the speed of reading, and ignoring the more important element of reading for understanding, has produced a large amount of concern in the literacy community (Allington, 2007; Newkirk, 2012).

For the purpose of having a common definition for the term fluency in this document, the following meaning from Timothy Rasinski will be used:

When readers embed appropriate volume, tone, emphasis, phrasing, and other elements in oral expression, they are giving evidence of actively interpreting or constructing meaning from the passage... (Rasinski, 2004, p 4)

Understanding the strong link between reading fluency and comprehension helps explain why middle and high school teachers will need to use some of their limited and valuable time to incorporate fluency instruction into their classes (Rasinski, 2004; Samuels, 1997). Just as the ultimate goal of all vocabulary instruction, word analysis and etymology instruction is to create better understanding, the purpose for integrating fluency lessons into the content area classrooms is to give students additional tools that will support the construction of meaning at deeper and deeper levels as they read.

Several practical applications for using fluency to enhance comprehension and word analysis skills are outlined later in this chapter.

The Needs of Adolescent Readers

Multiple teachers, restructured social groups, physical and emotional body changes, negative self-perception, increased behavior problems, higher independent academic expectations, and more sophisticated and complex textbook reading are some of the many transitional changes that take place as students progress from elementary school into middle school. Yet, perhaps, the problem with the most profound impact is that some students become disconnected and unmotivated readers when faced with almost complete independence of their own academic lives and the daunting task of structuring their own time and learning framework.

To add to the problem, teachers must also consider the multiple reading lives and complex communication systems students are facing every day on a social level. E-mail, smart phones, text messaging, **instant messaging**, social media....the list grows daily! The multitude of information that is instantly accessible on the internet, and even more information freely distributed through blogs and amateur websites, creates an exchange of information at a rate humans have never before experienced. And yet, teachers must in some way compete with these multiple reading lives while asking students to read content and classical instructional material for school.

What about adolescent students who struggle with the level of sophistication and difficulty of the text material placed before them? Many times there is a wide chasm between the expectations of elementary teachers and middle level teachers about the level of reading students should have gained before they enter middle school. As students progress through elementary school, they have continuing reading instruction every year in the early grades. Typically, teachers of kindergarten through third grade can be found using strategically scaffolded instruction and closely matched leveled texts to help students learn to navigate the process of beginning to read, then move them into the process of reading more and more difficult content area text (Allington, 2007). However, in the upper elementary school grades, the content curriculum becomes much more demanding of their time, and many teachers seem to perceive their students are able to read with adequate skill. A breakdown in understanding occurs when students are able to read fiction material with fluency, or even as "fake readers" who appear to be strong readers. These students act and talk like readers, but do not actually have the structures in place that will move them to become deeper readers when faced with more challenging material, but teachers of grades four and five may have the misperception that students can independently negotiate the harder text material without explicit reading instruction (Guthrie & Davis, 2003) and at this level direct instruction often seems to taper off.

The Need for Better Teacher Preparation

It is problematic that many middle and high school teachers report they have not had the educational background necessary to use reading instruction to help struggling readers. Although some teacher education programs for middle and high school teachers have a class for reading in the content area classes, teachers continue to report they do not have the pedagogy necessary for the monumental task that teachers of adolescents are being asked to do in CCSS.

It is even more problematic that some middle and high school teachers seem to have the attitude they do not want to learn to incorporate literacy into their classrooms, making statements such as "teaching reading is not my job". It would be unfathomable for any teacher to recognize that students struggle to read texts in their classroom without making an attempt to give the support those students need to read the texts. Lucy Calkins writes, *"Teach the writer, not the writing,"* so perhaps teachers of middle and high school students can learn to "*teach the learner, not the textbook*." Teachers who are tied to a curriculum or textbook may be adhering to the antiquated position they are expected to *cover* the material, and it is the job of students to *grasp* the material put before them.

How can teachers equip themselves to build the pedagogy needed to be more proficient teachers of reading? If educators want students to become deep thinkers about what they read, as the Common Core State Standards demand, perhaps the first step is to practice this as adult learners. If we want to create a generation of lifelong learners, we as a profession must also become lifelong learners. We must become a nation of adult learners, preferably in professional learning communities (PLC) with other educators, or, at the least, find a partner teacher who is like-minded, and begin a book study with high level discussion. We know that adolescent learners are social learners, so we must read and talk together, and analyze the evidence of how students learn. As adult learners we must discuss and process the information with other learners to gain deeper understanding and different perspectives. We must create a "culture of learning" in the classroom that acknowledges the necessity and value of more student talking and less teacher talking.

Rasinski (2004) wrote that students will learn what teachers teach, and because reading fluency has generally been thought of as within the domain of the elementary grades, it is unlikely that fluency will be taught explicitly or systematically in the middle and secondary grades unless a deliberate effort is made to educate reading, language arts, and English teachers. Unless this happens, students who lack sufficient fluency entering the middle grades are not likely to find the needed instructional support for their difficulties.

Motivating Adolescent Readers

Teachers of adolescents know that skill alone is rarely an incentive to motivate students to read material they don't want to read. There is a whole population of students who clearly possess the ability and skills necessary to read the assigned material, but still they continue to resist reading. Motivation, engagement, and attitude toward reading have been found to be as important as skill in encouraging adolescent students to read (Whittington, 2012). These capable but non-reading students have been given several different labels. Alvermann (2005) called them alliterate, and they have also been called reluctant readers, resistant readers, marginalized and disengaged readers (Fisher & Ivey, 2006; Ivey & Broaddus, 2001).

The reasons students do not read are numerous and multilayered. Lack of interest in the reading material teachers assign is the reason adolescents most often give about why they do not read, along with lack of choice in reading material (Whittington 2012). Realistically, it is not always possible to give students high interest materials in all classes, nor is it possible to always give a choice in what students are assigned to read. Some literature and content texts are mandated to be taught and this has traditionally been taught in large group settings. But, it may be much more productive that teachers alternate those non-negotiable assignments with high interest or self-selected reading material students, possibly from a controlled set of three or four texts a teacher has previously chosen. All readers within any classroom are never reading at the same level, so the option of allowing students to choose within a set will also allow the teacher to have some control over planning for students to have reading material that is at the appropriate learning level for them, rather than using the "one size fits all readers" approach that has most often been used in the past. Being able to choose their own reading material and work in a highly engaging environment seem to be key components to keeping adolescent students reading successfully and willing to work to increase their own skill (Ivey & Broaddus, 2001).

Another intervention any teacher can use is the methodology with which the content material is introduced. The fluency activities discussed later outline multiple ways content can be presented and practiced in any classroom. Another excellent resource for teachers is a publication by Fisher, Brozo, Frey, & Ivey (2006) entitled 50 Content Area Strategies for Adolescent Literacy, which gives multiple activities for immediate use in classrooms.

It is highly motivating for adolescents to use technology for learning and practice, and teachers can take advantage of the multiple text lives of students. For example, the media students read and the methods they report back information to the teacher can alternate with traditional paper and pencil activities for text quizzes or class email accounts. Gaggle accounts, Classchatter.com, or HomeworkNow.com are a few examples of sites that allow teachers to set up special class email accounts. Pole Everywhere and Text The Mob are sites that allow students to text answers to the teacher during class.

Middle and high school teachers must be aware of another concerning pattern of social behavior that often happens with both proficient and struggling readers during the adolescent years. Fink and

Samuels (2007) write that middle school students are likely to demonstrate self-handicapping strategies which impede their academic progress. For example, an adolescent might procrastinate and deliberately avoid reading and studying for a test; therefore, he can blame the low grade he receives on lack of studying instead of admitting he did not understand the concepts. By avoiding reading and other academic tasks, students can protect their self-image and social status with peers, thus poor reading achievement can be attributed to putting forth little effort or other socially accepted reasons, rather than their lack of intelligence, intellectual ability, and individual self-worth.

Students, Like Teachers, Learn Best in Community

Given the social nature of adolescent learners, instruction that incorporates social interaction through discussion and group work is a successful way to instruct middle school students on fluency. Common Core State Standards demand that students discuss and write arguments that are evidence based, and collaborative learning has been highly effective in teaching better metacognitive skills, listening skills, and learning to elaborate on meaning to defend a position (Marzano, 1992).

Working in a low stress setting, students are more likely to be able to safely help each other and to be engaged. Schmoker (2009) contends that dramatically increasing the amount of purposeful reading, writing, and discussion in all classrooms, content area classes as well as language arts classes, along with giving students interesting text material in which they can have the chance to discuss and argue about the characters and issues, will always increase their understanding of the material.

Prosody Instruction Enhances Fluency

The term prosody is new for many people, but affects the understanding of language each time a person speaks and reads. Exactly what is prosody? Prosody is an important element of reading that is associated with fluency and in the last few years, the term has gained more attention as an important contribution to proficient and fluent reading (Schwanenflugel, et al., 2006). One way to understand prosody is to use an analogy. Most people have received an email in which it was not clear if the writer was being sarcastic or funny, angry or facetious. It was difficult to tell the tone of the writer because the prosody was missing from that email.

Torgesen and Hudson (2006) best described prosody somewhat poetically as the "music" of oral language that signals question, surprise, exclamation and other meanings that change the semantics of the words being read. To say that prosody is the rhythm or music of language helps illustrate the need for appropriate phrasing, pausing and rate of reading in order for the text to be completely understood by both the reader and the listener.

Fluency and prosody instruction help students become more metacognitive, or know themselves as readers, which is an important and necessary practice used by proficient readers, and embedded throughout the Common Core State Standards. A student who is metacognitive in his reading will understand when meaning breaks down (Harvey & Goudvis, 2005) and will stop to use fix-up strategies that support his understanding of the text rather than continuing to "plow through" the words without understanding what he is reading.

Putting This Information Into Classroom Practice

There are several short and engaging activities that are highly motivating for students, and typically yield fairly quick results. Fluency instruction yields a lot of "bang for the buck." Fortunately, fluency instruction does not take a lot of time, nor does it take a great deal of direct instruction to increase fluent reading among adolescent readers.

Keep in mind the important motivational elements in allowing students to be able to choose their own reading material when possible, and to learn in social settings with collaboration involved in the activity. By having a selection of 3 or more possible choices from which to pick and allowing students to work with a partner or group, teachers will gain much in the area of motivating reluctant students to participate in the activities below.

Having direct teacher feedback is often the difference in how effective the activity shows increased results, so teachers will be well served to find a system with which they can periodically hear each student and give feedback about their growth.

Classroom Activities That Increase Fluency and Prosody

Repeated Reading Instruction:
   Reading a passage 3-5 times has strong value to increase both automaticity and prosody, as well as create stronger comprehension. Simply rereading is not motivating for students, but creating a purpose such as performance reading adds the motivation element.

   However, a very important word of caution: There is a fine line between using speed as a positive way to increase smooth reading, prosody and automaticity, and inadvertently giving the message that fast reading is always good reading. There must be a balance in the amount of timed reading and instruction on prosody, so students will not mistakenly learn the lesson they must read fast in order to read well. (Newkirk, 2012)

Repeated Reading Performance Instructional Activities:
   - **Poetry**
     Poetry reading with a partner is a very safe and low stress way to begin to increase fluency speed and automaticity. Having students time each other through 3-5 readings of a poem, giving constructive feedback to each other while the teacher is also providing feedback is an excellent way to increase fluency and speed of automaticity. The design of poetry, short phrases or sentences, allows readers quick success.

     Examples of Poetry for Adolescent Reading:
     The Road Not Taken by R. Frost

I Know Why the Caged Bird Sings by M. Angelou
O Captain, My Captain! by W. Whitman
A Red, Red Rose by R. Burns
Forgetfulness by B. Colllins
To a Daughter Leaving Home by L. Pastan
The Raven by E. A. Poe
How Do I Love Thee? By E. B. Browning
Be Glad Your Nose is on Your Face by J. Prelutsky
The Lorax by Dr. Seuss

Websites for Free Poetry:
http://www.poemhunter.com/poems/
http://www.poets.org/page.php/prmID/59
http://www.loc.gov/poetry/180/p180-list.html

Sample Assessment Rubric:
http://www.stowe.k12.vt.us/SMS/////teachers/sbuzzell/Homework%202011%202012/documents/poemreadingrubric.pdf

http://www.readwritethink.org/files/resources/lesson_images/lesson78/poetrubric.html

- **Readers Theater**
  Performance reading using Readers Theater is another low stress and safe way to provide fluency instruction and repeated reading. Readers Theater is engaging and motivating because it also incorporates social skills of collaborating with others. Many readers theater scripts can be found online free of charge.

Timothy Rasinski has an entire series of resource books published by Teacher Created Materials ready to use for fluency instruction, as well as several resources on his website at www.timrasinski.com.

Examples of Readers Theater for Adolescents:
- The Three Little Javelinas by S. Lowell
- Double Trouble in Walla Walla by A. Clements
- The True Story of the 3 Little Pigs by J. Shieszka
- And the Dish Ran Away with the Spoon by J. and S. Crummel
- A Christmas Carol by C. Dickens
- Dog Breath (The Horrible Trouble with Hally Tosis) by D. Pilkey
- The Great Kapok Tree by L. Cherry
- Where Once There Was a Wood by D. Fleming
- The Miracle Worker by W. Gibson
- Casey at the Bat by E.L. Thayer
- Greek Myths: Eros and Psyche

Resources for Readers Theater Scripts:

http://www.readinglady.com/index.php?module=documents&JAS_DocumentManager_op=viewDocument&JAS_Document_id=9&MMN_position=34:34

http://www.timelessteacherstuff.com/

http://www.teachingheart.net/readerstheater.htm

http://www.teachervision.fen.com/drama/literature/55301.html

http://www.readerstheaterallyear.com/ca
tegories/20100721_1

Sample Assessment Rubric:
http://www.readwritethink.org/classroom
-resources/printouts/readers-theatre-
rubric-30698.html

Sample Peer Assessment of Readers Theater:
http://www.teachervision.fen.com/tv/prin
tables/07AAAM42.pdf

One resource book for Readers Theater and 49 other activities for adolescent readers is published by Prentice Hall and entitled:
50 Content Area Strategies for Adolescent Literacy by Fisher, Brozo, Frey, & Ivey.

- **Famous American Speeches**
  The author used sections of Famous American Speeches found online at the following resources to successfully motivate students through fluency and repeated reading activities (Whittington, 2012).

  CCSS skills can easily be incorporated using famous American speeches in history and social studies reading, writing, and speaking when students research and share the historical implications of the context and setting of the speeches.

  Example of Excerpts from Famous Speeches:
  Inaugural Address, J.F. Kennedy
  I Have a Dream, M.L. King
  Gettysburg Address, A. Lincoln

Acceptance Speech, B. Obama
On Women's Right to Vote, S.B. Anthony
The Hypocrisy of American Slavery, F. Douglass
Liberty or Death, P. Henry

Websites for Famous Speeches:
http://www.biblicalpatriot.net/HistoricSpe
echesIndex.htm
http://www.historyplace.com/speeches/p
revious.htm
http://www.americanrhetoric.com/top100
speechesall.html

- **Historical Songs**
  Reading historical songs to teach fluency is a great way to practice fluency and prosody, as well as learning the context in which the song was written. Timothy Rasinski, a leading researcher and presenter in fluency instruction, has a resource ready to use for instruction of historical songs published by Teacher Created Materials. More information can be found at his website at timrasinski.com under Products. Free downloads can also be found online at several sources.

  Examples of Songs that Teach History:
  Battle of New Orleans, by Jimmy Driftwood
  The Ballad of Casey Jones, by Saunders, Seibert, and Newton.
  The Star Spangled Banner, by F. S. Key
  Brother Can You Spare a Dime? by E.Y. Harburg and J. Gorney

Websites for Historical Songs:
http://artsedge.kennedy-center.org/students/features/series/story-behind-the-song.aspx

http://parlorsongs.com/issues/2002-7/thismonth/feature.php

Prosody Instruction:
Phrasing, pausing, expression, inflection, pitch, and intonation are some of the elements of oral language that are included in prosody. Some students intrinsically understand that the expression used to read a selection changes the meaning of the words, but most students need to have explicit instruction to understand this abstract concept. Teaching students to be metacognitive, or thoughtful of their own thinking, helps them to understand that the way in which they read a selection aloud can change the meaning understood by the listener.

Activity1: One activity that can help students understand prosody is to show inflection of different words in a sentence. Each word in the sentence below can be stressed to show different meanings:

> ➢ <u>Sam</u> didn't say the girls moved the yellow crayon. (The word "Sam" is stressed, insinuating that someone said it, but it was not Sam.)
> ➢ Sam <u>didn't</u> say the girls moved that yellow crayon. (Denial)
> ➢ Sam didn't <u>say</u> the girls moved that yellow crayon. (Sam didn't say it, but it is insinuated that he thought it.)

- ➤ Sam didn't say the <u>girls</u> moved that yellow crayon. (Someone moved it, but it wasn't' the girls.)
- ➤ Sam didn't say the girls <u>moved</u> that yellow crayon. (The girls did something with the crayon, but they didn't move it.)
- ➤ Sam didn't say the girls moved <u>that</u> yellow crayon. (It is insinuated they moved another crayon.)
- ➤ Sam didn't say the girls moved that <u>yellow</u> crayon. (They moved a crayon, but not the yellow one.)
- ➤ Sam didn't say the girls moved that yellow <u>crayon</u>. (They moved something that was yellow. Perhaps a pencil? Pen?)

Have students practice with a sentence or poem, noticing how the meaning can change with different inflection and stress.

Example poems for prosody practice:
Bleezer's Ice Cream by J. Prelutsky (Humorous)
Super Sampson Simpson by J. Prelutsky (Humorous)
Bear in There by S. Silverstein (Humorous)
Science Homework by K. Nesbitt (Humorous)
Hey, Ma, There's Something Under My Bed by J. Horton (Humorous)
Adventures of Isabel by O. Nash (Humorous)
Annabel Lee by E.A. Poe (Classical)
No Man is an Island by J. Donne (Classical)
How Do I Love Thee? By E.B. Browning (Classical)

Resource for poems:
http://www.poemhunter.com/poets/
www.giggleppoetry.com

Activity 2: Listen to the audio version of a famous American speech, such as Martin Luther King, Jr.'s "I Have a Dream" speech. Stop and notice the way he stresses different words, pauses in certain places, uses inflection to show expression, etc. Practice with segments of speeches.

Website for audio of speeches:
http://www.americanrhetoric.com/top100speechesall.html

Phrase Instruction:

- Activity 1: Many students need instruction to read in phrases. An analogy that is fun to use with students is to talk like a computer (or find an audio of a computer speaking), and have students notice the lack of phrasing, and the resulting lack of meaning.
- Activity 2: Timothy Rasinski has a list of Fry's 600 Instant Phrases, based on Fry's Instant Word lists, on the website below. Practicing these phrases can help students learn better phrasing as they read.
  http://www.timrasinski.com/presentations/fry_600_instant_phrases.pdf
- Activity 3: Helping students notice that punctuation will help them have better phrasing and prosody, and in turn convey meaning in a better way.
  Have students read the following sentences and discuss how punctuation changes the meaning of each sentence. Have students try writing their own sentences:

- Let's eat Mommy. (Who is eating whom?)
- Let's eat, Mommy. (To whom is the author speaking?)

- My dog, Riley, is a fun travel companion. (Who is a fun travel companion?)
- My dog Riley is a fun travel companion. (Who is a fun travel companion?)

- Sara Elizabeth, John Michael, and I will play baseball. (How many people will play baseball?)
- Sara, Elizabeth, John, Michael, and I will play baseball. (How many people will play baseball?)

> ➤ Sylvia, Scott is going to make the cake for
> the party. (Who is making the cake?)

> ➤ Sylvia Scott is going to make the cake for
> the party. (Who is making the cake?)

- Read aloud and discuss: <u>Eats, Shoots, & Leaves</u> by Lynne Truss, in which missing or misplaced commas create comical situations.

Paired Reading or Reading Partners:
Adolescents are social learners, and paired reading is a great way to practice fluency and prosody with a purpose. It is especially effective to have weak adolescent readers read aloud to a younger or less proficient reader. Setting up a partnership with a lower grade or different group to partner once per week for reading will typically yield strong results in reading proficiency of both groups of students (Topping, 1989).

Concluding Thoughts

Although fluency instruction is only one of the important areas of literacy intervention, giving students support in learning to be more fluent readers has a strong correlation with increased achievement in comprehension. As students become adept at using prosody to convey the intended meaning, and become more automatic in retrieving the necessary words while reading, they are freeing up more brain power for synthesizing the large amount of information they will face as middle school readers in an age of information technology.

Many teachers report they are feeling attacked from all sides to make rapid changes in curriculum regarding the way they teach their given content area, while concurrently learning to be teachers of reading. One action every teacher can take is to become proactive in educating himself or herself about literacy instruction for adolescents. Below are several very teacher-friendly books that will help construct a foundation on which to build more professional knowledge about literacy.

It is assumed that each teacher wishes to deliver the best education possible for his or her students. Therefore, collaborating with other teachers about information from the resources below, or other credible resources, is a solid first step in showing good faith effort to become current in research based best practice instructional methodology in helping students to be more fluent and more prosodic adolescent readers.

Resources for Further Reading for Teachers of Adolescents:

50 Content Area Strategies for Adolescent Literacy. Fisher, D., Brozo, W., Frey, N., & Ivey G. (2006). New York: Prentice Hall.

Genre Connections: Lessons to Launch Literacy and Nonfiction Texts. McGregor, T. (2013). Portsmouth, NH: Heinemann.

I Read It, But I Don't Get It. Tovani, C. (2000). Portland: Stenhouse Publishers.

Text and Lessons for Content-Area Reading. Daniels, H., and Steineke, N. (2011). Portsmouth, NH: Heinemann.

The Comprehension Toolkit. Harvey, S., & Goudvis A. (2005). Portsmouth, NH: Heinemann.

When Kids Can't Read---What Teachers Can Do. Beers, K. (2002). Portsmouth, NH: Heinemann Publishers.

References:

Allington, R. (1983). Fluency: The neglected goal. *The Reading Teacher*. 36, 556-561.

Allington, R. (2000). *What really matters for struggling readers.* Boston: Allyn & Bacon.

Allington, R. (2007). Intervention all day long: New hope for struggling readers. *Voices From the Middle, 14*(4), 7-15.

Alvermann, D. (2005). Literacy on the edge: How close are we to closing the literacy achievement gap? *Voices From the Middle, 13*(1), 8-15.

Beers, K. (2002). *When kids can't read---What teachers can do.* Portsmouth, NH: Heinemann Publishers.

Calkins, L. (1999). Let the words work their magic. *Instructor, 110*(3), 25-29.

Fisher, D., Brozo, W., Frey, N., & Ivey G. (2006). *50 content area strategies for adolescent literacy*. New York: Prentice Hall.

Fisher, D., & Ivey, G. (2006). Evaluating the interventions for struggling adolescent readers. *Journal of Adolescent & Adult Literacy, 50*(3), 180-190.

Guthrie, J., & Davis, M. (2003). Motivating struggling readers in middle school through an engagement model of classroom practice. *Reading & Writing Quarterly, 19*, 59-85.

Harvey, S., & Goudvis A. (2005). *The Comprehension Toolkit.* Portsmouth, NH: Heineman.

International Reading Association and the National Middle School Association (2001). Supporting young adolescent's literacy learning: A joint position statement of the International Reading Association and the National Middle School Association, Dec 2001

Ivey, G., & Broaddus, K. (2001). "Just plain reading": A survey of what makes students want to read in middle school classrooms. *Reading Research Quarterly, 36*(4), 350–377.

Kamil, M. L., Borman, G. D., Dole, J., Kral, C. C., Salinger, T., and Torgesen, J. (2008). *Improving adolescent literacy: Effective classroom and intervention practices: A Practice Guide* (NCEE #2008-4027). Washington, DC: National Center for Education Evaluation and Regional Assistance, Institute of Education Sciences, U.S. Department of Education.

Marzano, Robert, (1992). The many faces of cooperation across the dimensions of learning, in *Enhancing Thinking Through Cooperative Learning*. Edited by Davidson and Worsham. New York: Teachers College Press.

National Reading Panel (2000). *Report of the National Reading Panel: Teaching children to read, report of the subgroups.* Washington, DC: National Institute of Child and Health and Development.

Newkirk, T. (2011.) *The Art of Slow Reading.* Portsmouth, NH: Heinemann Publishers.

Nichols, W., Rupley, W., & Rasinski, T. (2009) Fluency in learning to read for meaning: Going beyond repeated readings. *Literacy Research and Instruction, 48*(1), 1-14.

Pressley, M., Gaskins, I., & Fingeret, L. (2006). Instruction and development of reading fluency in struggling readers. In J. Samuels & A. Farstrup (Eds.) *What research has to say about fluency instruction* (pp. 47-69). Newark, DE: International Reading Association.

Rasinski, T. (2004). *Assessing reading fluency.* Honolulu: Pacific Resources for Education and Learning.

Rasinski, T., Rikli, A., & Johnston, S. (2009). Reading fluency: More than automaticity? More than a concern for the primary grades? *Literacy Research and Instruction, 48*(4), 350-361.

Robb, L. (2002). The myth: Learn to read/read to learn. *Scholastic Instructor, 111*(8) 23-25.

Samuels, S. (1997). Introduction to automaticity: Theory and practice. *Reading and Writing Quarterly, 13*(2) 103-105.

Schmoker, M. (2009). What money can't buy: Powerful, overlooked opportunities for learning. *Phi Delta Kappan,* 90, (7) 524-528.

Schwanenflugel, P., Meisinger, E., Wisenbaker, J., & Kuhn, M. (2006). Becoming a fluent and automatic reader in the early elementary school years. *Reading Research Quarterly, 41*(4), 496-519.

Topping, K. (1989). Peer tutoring and paired reading: Combining two powerful techniques. *The Reading Teacher, 42*(7), 488-494.

Tovani, C. (2000). *I read it, but I don't get it.* Portland: Stenhouse Publishers.

Whittington, M. (2012). Motivating adolescent readers: A middle school reading fluency and prosody intervention. ProQuest, UMI Dissertations Publishing, 2012. 3519114.

Manufactured by Amazon.ca
Bolton, ON